THE ANAYA **SUN SIGN** *COMPANIONS*

SCORPIO

24 October-22 November

CELESTINE O'RYAN

ANAYA PUBLISHERS LIMITED
LONDON

First published in Great Britain in 1991 by
Anaya Publishers Ltd., Strode House, 44-50 Osnaburgh Street, London NW1 3ND

Copyright © Anaya Publishers Ltd 1991

ASTROLOGICAL CONSULTANT Jan Kurrels

Managing Editor	Judy Martin
Art Director	Nigel Osborne
Designers	Sally Stockwell
	Anne Clue
Illustrators	Marion Appleton
	David Ashby
	Lorraine Harrison
	Tony Masero
Indexer	Peter Barber

British Library Cataloguing in Publication Data
O'Ryan, Celestine
   Scorpio. – (Anaya sun sign companions).
   1. Astrology
   I. Title
   133.52
   ISBN 1-85470-097-9

TYPESET IN GREAT BRITAIN BY MIDFORD TYPESETTING LTD, LONDON
COLOUR ORIGINATION IN SINGAPORE BY COLUMBIA OFFSET LTD
PRINTED IN SINGAPORE BY TIMES OFFSET LTD

CONTENTS

SCORPIO

*Most people know their own sun sign, and you know
that yours is Scorpio, but do you appreciate its full
impact on every area of your life? Your* Sun Sign
Companion *is a guide to the many pleasures
and preferences that are specific to you as a
Scorpio subject.*
*Your personality profile is here – and much more. You
can find out not only where you fit into the grand
astrological scheme and the ways the other zodiac signs
connect with your own, but also discover the delights of
the Scorpionic foods that are your special delicacies; the
plants that you should grow in your garden to enhance
your Scorpionic moods; the animals that you
appreciate for their affinities to your sign and the pets
that you as a Scorpio can easily love and live with; the
ways in which you need to take care of your body, and
how your health and well-being may be affected by the
fact that you were born under Scorpio.*

The fascinating range of this Sun Sign Companion *explains your temperament, your actions and the ways you live your life in zodiacal terms. You are intense and self-disciplined and your special element – water – is the element of life itself; your planetary ruler Pluto, lord of the underworld, strengthens your emotional resources and determination to succeed. You have singular connections with the powers of the Earth itself – its gemstones, metals and crystals. And your zodiacal profile is underlined by your Scorpionic connections to the ancient arts of the Runes and the Tarot.*

This book provides you with the intriguing mosaic of influences, interests and attributes that build into the total picture of yourself as a Scorpio. More than any other zodiacal guide, your Sun Sign Companion *reveals to you the inherent fun and enjoyment of life under Scorpio.*

S C O R P I O
THE ZODIAC

hen the ancient astrologers studied the sky at night, they tracked the obvious motion and changing shape of the Moon, but noted two other phenomena: the frosty grandeur of the fixed stars and the different movements of the five observable planets. Mercury, Venus, Mars, Jupiter and Saturn moved and weaved about the night sky in repeating patterns, always within the same narrow strip of the heavens. And in the day time, the Sun could be seen progressing along the centre of this strip on its apparent orbit. Most of the action, celestially speaking, appeared to take place in a restricted

heavenly corridor. Astronomers and astrologers therefore gave priority to this ribbon of sky, and noted what else appeared in it.

Sharing the strip were twelve fixed star constellations, known from ancient times. They were Aries the Ram, Taurus the Bull, Gemini the Twins, Cancer the Crab, Leo the Lion, Virgo the Virgin, Libra the Balance, Scorpius the Scorpion, Sagittarius the Archer, Capricornus the Goat, Aquarius the Water Carrier and Pisces the Fishes. As most of the constellations are named after sentient creatures, the Greeks called this band of sky the zodiac, from their word meaning images of animals or living beings.

In astronomical terms, the constellations take up varying amounts of sky and exhibit different degrees of brightness. Astrologically, they are assigned equal prominence and importance, and are given equal 30-degree arcs of the celestial band. These are the signs of the zodiac, and the starting point on the celestial circle is 0 degrees Aries, which was the point of the vernal equinox over 4000 years ago when the zodiac was established.

The celestial jostling along the zodiacal corridor is explained by the fact that the planets orbit the Sun roughly in the same plane. Imagine yourself at the centre of a race track, timing a group of runners as they lap the circuit, each one running at a different pace and in a different lane. Soon you would be able to predict when each one would pass you, especially if you noted down landmarks along the spectator stands behind the runners.

In the same way, astrologers pinpoint the position and motion of any planet, using the zodiac band as a reference grid. Interpretation of the effects of planetary power filtered through the zodiac grid is the enduring fascination of astrology. The planets are extremely powerful, as represented by their having been awarded the names and attributes of the gods.

ZODIACAL INFLUENCES

our sun sign is the zodiac sign that the Sun, the most powerful of the heavenly bodies, appears to be passing through from our viewpoint on Earth at the time of your birth. It takes the Sun one year to progress through all the signs, and it is the Sun's huge power, filtered through each sign in turn, that etches the broad character templates of the signs. Over the centuries, each sign has acquired its own repertory of characteristics and personality traits, a seamless blend of archetypal myth and particular observation. So now we can talk about, say, a 'typical Scorpio' with the expectation that others will know what we mean. However, fine tuning and modification of the individual personality are dictated by two conditions at the time of birth – the positions of the Moon and planets in the zodiac and the nature of the ascendant, the sign rising on the eastern horizon at the moment of birth.

The Earth spins counter-clockwise daily on its axis, but to us it appears that the Sun, stars and planets wheel overhead from east to west. Within this framework, the zodiac passing overhead carries with it one sign every two hours; therefore the degree of the ascendant changes likewise, which explains why two people born on the same day can have such varying personalities. The influence of the ascending sign, and any planet positioned in it, has a strong bearing on the formation of the personality. A Scorpio with Pisces in the ascendant is quite a different kettle of fish to one with Capricorn ascending.

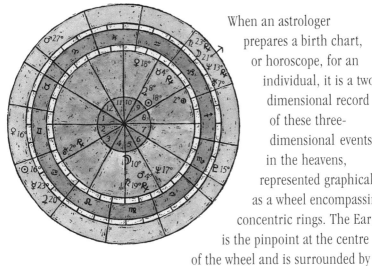

When an astrologer prepares a birth chart, or horoscope, for an individual, it is a two-dimensional record of these three-dimensional events in the heavens, represented graphically as a wheel encompassing concentric rings. The Earth is the pinpoint at the centre of the wheel and is surrounded by twelve fixed segments representing the zodiacal Houses, the areas of life in which planetary influences will manifest themselves. The outer circle of the chart represents the moving zodiacal corridor, divided into its twelve segments – the signs of the zodiac.

The predictability of the planets' movements has enabled astrologers to create tables, known as Ephemerides, of the planetary positions past, present and future. Once the positions of the Sun, Moon and planets have been established for a specific time, and a particular subject, the astrologer can assess and interpret what effects the planets will have, how they will enhance, diminish or frustrate each other's powers, and which areas of the subject's life will come under their particular influences. And all of this information is blended with the astrologer's understanding of the sun sign personality, the broad framework of individuality in zodiacal terms.

THE SCORPIO PERSONALITY

 corpio is the eighth sign of the zodiac. Brooding, magnetic and intense, Scorpios are a puzzle to the other zodiac signs: they seem to be connected to some invisible power source inaccessible to the rest of us. They can direct their energies into any field, with a high expectation of success. Fiercely determined, brave, self-disciplined and entirely self-motivated, Scorpios are certain of their own judgements and need no approval from others for their projects and plans – especially business plans. They understand the ebb and flow of big money markets and can become obscenely wealthy if they put their minds to it. The formidable Scorpio intellect slices through problems that leave others enmeshed and floundering, and their cool, penetrating stare seems able to see through other people's protective layers to the essence within. Such power can have an aphrodisiac effect: not for nothing is Scorpio reputed to be the sexiest sign of the zodiac.

Scorpio's secret is the deep, dark pool of emotions carried within; outwardly calm, Scorpios give away no secrets while bringing a high emotional charge to everything they do – work, rest, play and love life. Mediocrity is unacceptable to Scorpio. Moody and magnificent Scorpios can sink into black despair, and it is a brave friend that will make the attempt to bring them back. But it is not all brooding gloom: Scorpios also love the good things in life – food, drink, music, art, friendship – and their trenchant wit makes them entertaining company.

Scorpio
Orbis Regens Pluto
Signum Obstans Taurus

THE PLANETARY RULER

ncient astrologers named the five planets they could see in the night sky after the five most powerful classical gods; naturally, the planets took on the attributes and associations of the gods, and a pleasingly symmetrical system was devised to distribute this planetary power throughout the zodiac.

The Sun and Moon, being the most dazzling lights, ruled one sun sign each (Leo and Cancer). The remaining ten signs managed under the shared patronage of the five planets. Mercury presided over Gemini and Virgo, Venus over Taurus and Libra, Mars over Aries and Scorpio, Jupiter over Sagittarius and Pisces, and Saturn over Aquarius and Capricorn.

When more planets were discovered after the invention of the telescope in 1610, a reshuffle became necessary. Uranus (discovered in 1781) was allocated to Aquarius, Neptune (1836) was thought appropriate for Pisces, and Pluto (1930) now broods

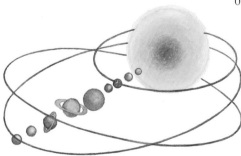

over Scorpio. This has unbalanced the symmetry: the search is on for other planets to share the burden with Venus and Mercury. Indeed, the asteroid Chiron, discovered in 1977 looping the void between Saturn and Uranus, is considered by some astrologers to be the suitable governor of Virgo.

The planetary power behind Scorpio is now attributed to Pluto, lord of the underworld. Originally, Scorpio was assigned to Mars, but this dynamic, active planet never seemed entirely to explain

 the complex, introverted Scorpio persona, although Martian will and determination are certainly strong Scorpionic traits. On the positive side, Pluto indicates a sharp analytical mind, the ability to amass wealth, the courage to make irrevocable changes, the emotional resource to weather the seismic events in life, to stare destruction in the face and soar above it. Adversely it can signal an underhand ability to manipulate business and financial power to bad ends and the capacity to embrace degradation, to sink to life's lowest depths without disintegrating.

Astronomically, Pluto is the ninth and smallest planet in the solar system. According to current thinking, it is a dense iceberg, no bigger than our Moon. Pluto takes 246 years to orbit the Sun, and because its orbit is eccentric, it will sometimes deviate from the zodiac band.

In classical mythology, Pluto, brother of Zeus, is the king of Hades, the underworld, the zealous guardian of dead souls (the Romans called him Hades, or Dis). As owner of all the Earth's mineral riches, handsome Pluto cut a devilish swathe amongst the nymphs and goddesses on his sorties to the upper world, hidden by his helmet of invisibility. His most famous consort was Persephone, daughter of the earth goddess Demeter.

PATTERNS IN THE STARS

tar pictures, or images of the constellations, are formed in the eye of the beholder. What we see as a neighbourly cluster is usually an optical illusion, the stars in the group being many light years apart. Even so, the urge to impose a friendly pattern on the frosty immensity of the night sky, to link the stars with the myths and legends on Earth, has been irresistible to all cultures. Different cultures make out different pictures, and the results are sometimes inscrutable – searching for Leo, say, you will look in vain for the shape of a lion pricked out in stars against the dark backcloth of the night sky.

The zodiac constellations were among the first to be made out, as they were the star groups that formed the background to the moving planets, providing a useful reference grid to plot planetary movements. These gave their names to the signs of the zodiac, although they spread unevenly across the sky and are not tidily

confined to the equal 30-degree segments of the imaginary zodiac band. Most stars are known by their Arabic names, and the star that shone brightest in each constellation when Arabic astrologers first compiled their star catalogues was designated its alpha.

The constellation that gave its name to the eighth sign of the zodiac is one of the richest in the sky, the glorious southern star group Scorpius the Scorpion, an opulent rope of twenty bright stars glittering against the magnificence of the Milky Way. One of the few zodiacal constellations to bear even a passing resemblance to its namesake, Scorpius really does look like a scorpion, with a 'sting' in its magnificent 'tail' formed by the stars Shaula, Lesath and Girtab, and a glowering red heart, the mighty Antares, the 'rival of Mars'. Antares is the guardian of the western sky, one of a square of four bright, fixed stars called by Persian astronomers the Watchers of the Heavens. Scorpius is made even more splendid by several rich star clusters, visible to the naked eye and through binoculars.

Scorpius is the starry image of the mythical scorpion sent by Apollo to destroy Orion, the son of Poseidon and a mighty hunter. Orion had joined forces with Apollo's sister Artemis the Huntress and boasted that he could kill all the wild beasts on Earth. As patron of the animals and as brother to Artemis, whom he feared might fall for Orion's obvious charms, Apollo sent the death-dealing scorpion. The confrontation was inconclusive, so Apollo tricked Artemis into accidentally killing Orion. The remorseful goddess placed the hunter among the stars, whereupon Apollo elevated the scorpion as well; and the two are now locked in eternal pursuit around the heavens.

THE ATTRACTION OF OPPOSITES

 n astrological terms, polarity describes the strong complementary relationship between signs that are exactly opposite each other on the zodiac circle, 180 degrees or six signs apart. These signs share the same gender – masculine or feminine – and the same quality – cardinal, fixed or mutable – and so share the ways they look at the world and shape their energy. Characteristics and interests complement each other or harmonize on different scales.

Relationships between polar signs are often very satisfying and fruitful, especially in the context of work. A clue to this affinity lies with the elements governed by each sign. The mathematics of polarity mean that earth signs oppose only water signs, and that fire opposes only air. Fire and air signs therefore encourage and inspire each other – fire cannot burn without air and air needs heat to rise. Earth and water signs conspire together creatively – earth without water is unfruitful, water unconfined by earth wastes its energy in diffusion – and

together they make mud, rich material for any creative process.

Six signs away from brooding, magnetic, sexy Scorpio, the enigmatic loner of the zodiac, we find methodical, conventional Taurus, the very essence of corporate, cooperative man.

Honest, open Taurus, who contentedly toils his way through life's hierarchies without complaint, might invite the scorn of

mysterious Scorpio, whose life is shaped by unpredictable excesses, byzantine secrecy and passionate intensity.

Below the surface, however, a shared and complementary shaping energy is at work, the fixed energy of consolidation. Both Scorpio and Taurus preside over pivotal times of the year, when the seasonal die has been cast and the Earth is held in temporary balance. Everything is either inevitably growing towards fruition or retreating into dormancy. Scorpio, the water sign, is obsessed with gathering, storing and remembering emotional and spiritual experiences. Taurus, the earth sign, concerns itself with the getting, holding and keeping of material assets.

The complementary aspect of polarity is also seen in the characteristics traditionally associated with the two signs. Tenacity, accumulation and enclosure are common to both, but on very different levels. Whereas Scorpio stares deeply into an enclosed inner lake of feelings, Taurus is proudly surveying the neat hedgerows that mark out his property. Both are concerned with establishing the boundaries of existence, but in opposite directions: Scorpio deals with the inner self, the intangible and metaphysical; Taurus with the outer self, the tangible and immediate.

THE SYMBOLS OF THE ZODIAC

ver since astrology began, there has been a kind of astrological shorthand, a set of symbols or ideograms called glyphs. Glyphs make the language of astrology universal and available to people who have no literary tradition. They also make it easy to draw up a birth chart, being a convenient form of notation, especially where planets are clustered in one area of the chart.

Each of the zodiac signs has its own glyph, as do the planets. They have evolved over centuries, and so are now freighted with symbolism, not simply convenient codes.

Today, the glyph for Scorpio is a powerful graphic representation, an M-shaped symbol with an upcurving talon at the beginning and a lashing arrow-shaped tail at the end. The image has remained remarkably consistent through the ages, although its basis seems to be a serpent

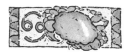

rather than a scorpion. Early Egyptians adopted a hieroglyph of a splendid cobra-like snake – the asp of Cleopatra – rearing up in a series of undulations. The Greek symbol adhered to the snake motif, being a simple serpentine loop, with a distinct cobra-hooded head at one end. Medieval astrologers had two versions, one an ornate flourish bearing a noticeable resemblance to the Egyptian model; the other an oblique double-looped spiral.

There is a special fascination in studying the glyphs to see what other symbolism may be contained within them. The rigid downstrokes of the M reflect Scorpio's strength of purpose, while the flow of the whole shape echoes the constant flow of life, from birth to death to birth again, that Scorpio understands. The arrow-shaped 'tail' emphasizes the penetrating quality of the powerful analytical Scorpio mind.

Planets also have their glyphs. Pluto has a modernist graphic combining the first two letters of the planet's name, a capital P with a horizontal line extending to the right from the base of the downstroke.

THE HOUSE OF SCORPIO

he twelve Houses are an intellectual concept, not a physical reality, an expression of all the aspects of human life and experience, from the self to the infinite. Each is associated with a sign of the zodiac, sharing its planetary ruler and elemental energy. However, the Houses are fixed and constant – they are represented by the central

numbered segments on a birth chart – and the signs and planets pass through them. They are the channels through which planetary and zodiacal energies flow and indicate which area of life is the focus of particular zodiacal influence at any one time.

Scorpio, being the eighth sign of the zodiac, is associated with the Eighth House, which is also overseen by Scorpio's planetary ruler Pluto. Like Scorpio, it is flooded with water energy, which means that it concerns itself with the life of the emotions and feelings. In particular, the Eighth House is concerned with the thrust of the life-force itself – vitality, sex, death and their attendant emotions; with the fascination of the secrets of the afterlife; and with the awesome power of serious money, as inheritance, big business or the fruits of crime. The Eighth House is an introverted, powerful

and rather intimidating place, somewhere to brood on the great mysteries of life, compile a wealth-generating portfolio of stocks and shares, or plot a devastating business coup.

When Pluto is in the Eighth House on a Scorpio birth chart, it magnifies the instinctive Scorpionic talent for incisive analysis, penetrating logic and perceptive intuition. It can also signal an auspicious time to think about long-term investments.

ELEMENTS AND QUALITIES

t was Aristotle, the great Greek thinker, who formalized the idea that all life is made up from infinitely various permutations of the four elements – fire, earth, air and water. In the zodiac cycle there are three signs representing each element. Aries, Leo and Sagittarius are for fire; Taurus, Virgo and Capricorn for earth; Gemini, Libra and Aquarius for air; and Cancer, Scorpio and Pisces for water.

However, in each case, the element is filtered through a different kind, or quality, of energy field; cardinal, fixed and mutable (or transforming). Aries, Cancer, Libra and Capricorn are cardinal; Taurus, Leo, Scorpio and Aquarius are fixed; Gemini, Virgo, Sagittarius and Pisces are mutable. Each sign is a unique manifestation of one element and one quality of energy.

Water is the Scorpio element; soothing, refreshing, cleansing, purifying, the essence of humanity – after all we are all seventy-two per cent water. Universally accepted as a metaphor for the mysterious unconscious mind, water is the indicator of moods, the signifier of the ebb and flow of being, the power that rocks the cradle of life itself. This is the element that can quench a thirst, irrigate a desert or savagely dash a ship to pieces on the rocks. Water at peace is a thing of serene, limpid beauty; water in turmoil is merciless and murderous. Scorpio has profound respect for the physical and spiritual powers of water; but the urge to exercise Scorpionic control may lead to a career as a lone yachtsperson.

Scorpio energy is fixed. Fixed energy people are the consolidators, the builders, the steadfast guardians of their particular energy. Scorpionic waters are still and run deep; the lake rather than the river. Anybody can ruffle the surface of the lake, but no one can ever plumb Scorpio's mysterious depths.

THE ZODIAC GARDEN

corpio speeding by in a mysterious black-windowed automobile, or striding along observing the rural life from behind mirrored sunglasses, cuts an incongruous dash in arcadia. Although Scorpios appreciate the food that is grown and raised there, they would rather be brooding by the edge of a deep, dark lake, or exploring the neglected and overgrown backwaters of an urban canal system.

When they make their money, however, Scorpios will really enjoy an extensive tour of Europe's vineyards and wine cellars.

The ideal garden for Scorpio is as enigmatic as its owner. Thick hedges or clumps of bushy trees – blackthorn, holly, hawthorn, viburnum, privet, hazel, box – may be arranged to make a secluded shrubbery for lovers or a labyrinthine plot-hatchery for conspirators. Scorpio would adore the byzantine convolutions of a maze, and may while away winter evenings designing one. Water is also essential – in the form of a lake for the plutocratic Scorpio, a pond or fountain for the aspiring scorpion. Another feature attractive to Scorpios is a secluded bog garden fringed with water-loving plants bearing the dark red flowers that Scorpio favours – crimson astilbes, bog pimpernels, pink and red bog primroses – or heady, exotic arum lilies, the flower of the *fin-de-siecle*. The path to this garden may be lined with shade-loving rhododendrons.

Scorpios will equally enjoy the formal scarlet delights of geraniums, pelargoniums and begonias. Rigid red tulips appeal to the disciplinarian in Scorpio. They can also appreciate the zen beauty of Japanese stone gardens that austerely consist of raked gravel and precisely placed rocks.

Keen to maintain the formal difference between house and garden, Scorpio opts for exotic indoor plants: orchids, perhaps, or fleshy-leaved aechmeas, or the mysterious night-flowering cactus. As for cut flowers, Scorpio would really like black ones; but sheaths of red gladioli or tall lilies create the formal style of arrangement that Scorpio admires.

ASTROLOGY AND THE ARK

he word zodiac comes from the Greek word for living creatures, and many of the signs are symbolized by animals. Scorpio is represented by the scorpion, a mysterious ancient animal that makes its nest underground and bears the seeds of destruction in its lashing, lethal tail, which it can, and occasionally does, turn suicidally on itself. However, ancient astrologers associated Scorpio with the eagle, the very symbol of soaring, far sighted nobility. The eagle in Scorpio (note the penetrating gaze of most Scorpios) thrills to the breathtaking sight of a great bird of prey on the wing.

Unsurprisingly, Scorpio the sign is primarily associated with crustaceans and insects. Like Scorpio, insects are an enigma: by far the most successful creatures on the planet, in terms of numbers, they live their busy frantic lives of birth, copulation and death hidden from human gaze. Yet their power is inexorable, as anyone who has ever witnessed the destruction that can be wrought by a locust swarm or a colony of ants will tell you.

Scorpios may well have an insectarium at home, a hand-made ant city where they can study micro-power struggles and the tiny rigid hierarchies at work. As they also take great, if secret, glee in shocking the staid, Scorpio may well appear with a pet rat or parrot clinging to one shoulder. It is the animal soul that fascinates Scorpio, not possession of their bodies; they are  uninterested in dogs (far too obvious) and prefer to commune with enigmatic, self-possessed, intuitive cats, especially black ones whose green glass eyes hold the secrets of the universe: and the connection of black cats with witches only makes them all the more fascinating.

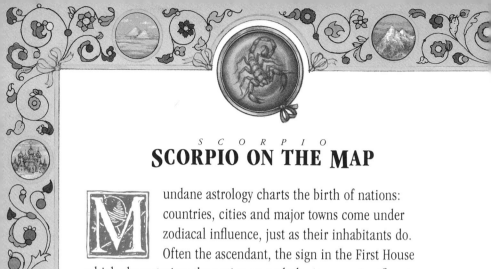

SCORPIO ON THE MAP

Mundane astrology charts the birth of nations: countries, cities and major towns come under zodiacal influence, just as their inhabitants do. Often the ascendant, the sign in the First House which characterizes the nation as a whole, is more significant than the sun sign. Various methods are used to assess which zodiac sign holds sway where. Countries with an incontestable birthday – 4 July 1776 for the USA, for instance – have a standard birth chart. In countries which have evolved more organically, zodiacal influences may be deduced by the broad characteristics – can you think of a more suitable ruling sign than Taurus for Switzerland, the land loud with cowbells? Cities and towns may show their zodiacal allegiance by their function – most spas are ruled by health-conscious Virgo, and the administrative heart of any capital city is ruled by Capricorn, the zodiac's bureaucrat.

Scorpio's worldly subjects include Morocco, Norway, Korea, and the Transvaal. Scorpios are seduced by the ancient sunbaked glamour of the Middle East. Morocco, bound on the north by the sea and in the south by the fierce Sahara desert, fascinates them particularly. In contrast, Norway, the Land of the Midnight Sun (a nice enigma for Scorpio) is fringed with fjords, secretive inlets of deep, still waters; it was from here that the lusty Vikings set sail on their worldwide adventures. Korea, the once-divided peninsula sustained by its mineral wealth and fishing industry, was once

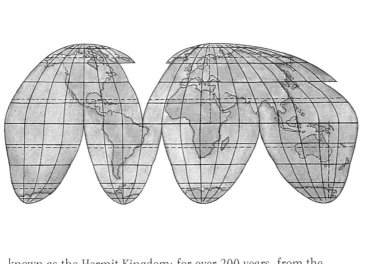

known as the Hermit Kingdom: for over 200 years, from the seventeenth century, it spurned all foreigners and turned in on itself to brood. South Africa's Transvaal provides enormous amounts of gold, enough to satisfy the most plutocratic scorpion.

Some cities under Scorpio emphasize the Moorish connection: Fez, the ancient traditional capital of Morocco and Valencia, the Moors' gateway to Spain. Others unite water and wealth, big-time ports that combine shipping, fishing and heavy industry, especially mining: Cincinnati, Liverpool, Hull, Newcastle-on-Tyne; Baltimore, city of steel; Milwaukee, the Great Lake port and Beer Capital of the USA; and New Orleans, the pearl of the Mississippi, world famous as the birthplace of jazz and fine creole cuisine – but also coloured by the superstitious cult of voodoo.

S C O R P I O

EARTH'S BOUNTY

 oods associated with Scorpio are onions, leeks, hops and red meat, an inheritance from Scorpio's former planetary ruler Mars which is shared with hot-blooded Aries. Onions and leeks keep the blood flowing healthily (stagnation brings Scorpio down) and red meat fuels Scorpionic (and Arian) action. There the similarity ends. Whereas Aries eats to live, Scorpio eats to experience: Scorpios are the experimental gourmets of the zodiac – and it doesn't take much to turn them into *gourmands*. Scorpios love the good

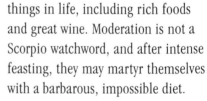

things in life, including rich foods and great wine. Moderation is not a Scorpio watchword, and after intense feasting, they may martyr themselves with a barbarous, impossible diet.

Scorpio's interest in food has no boundaries. Although Scorpios are particularly attracted to hot, spicy foods (Indian, Middle Eastern, Mexican), they also relish the exotic for its own sake and fearlessly confront foods that are unusual, even unpalatable to the majority. Eating with

Scorpio will always be an adventure: expect anything, from a gullet-scorching vindaloo curry to an exquisite fourteen-course Malayan supper, from raw fish with *akvavit* to a replica medieval banquet. And there will always be a mouth-watering dessert, probably involving a lot of cake.

Whatever you eat, the wine that is served with your food will be wonderful. Scorpios really understand wine, especially the reds. They appreciate the great vintages and the famous vineyards, but will delight in new discoveries from little known or unlikely sources – such as wines from Lebanon, Chile or Russia. To end the meal, you will get as memorable a port as Scorpio can afford.

Dining out with Scorpio is never dull; you will be taken to an unassuming Thai café for a real taste of the Far East, or to the only place in town that serves authentic couscous, or jambalaya, or curried goat. Scorpios haunt the wine bars and chophouses that feed the city's financial quarter, where the scent of big money hangs on the air. Power lunches – even other people's – intoxicate them.

A HEAVENLY HERBAL

erbs and the heavens have been linked forever; for many centuries, herbs were the only medicine, and the gathering and application of them were guided by the planets. Doctors would learn the rudiments of astrology as a matter of course – Hippocrates claimed that 'a physician without a knowledge of astrology had no right to call himself a physician'.

Healing plants and their ruling planets were often linked via the elements – fire, water, air and earth. Mars, for example, a hot fiery planet, self-evidently rules over hot, fiery plants such as mustard. Herbs that cure the ills of particular parts of the body are ruled by the planet that governs that part of the body. Plants are also assigned according to what they look like. For example, walnuts, which look like tiny models of the brain, are ruled by Mercury, the planet which rules the brain.

All herbs are more effective if they are gathered on a day ruled by their patron planet, especially at dawn, when they are fat with sap drawn up by the beams of the Moon, or at dusk, after a day basking in the strengthening rays of the Sun.

Scorpio culls a rich harvest from the herb garden, as it can lay claim to Martian herbs as well as its own, which are catnip, aloe and witchhazel. Catnip – more properly catmint – is the unassuming herb, once used as a base for home-made tonic, that drives cats crazy. (One of Pluto's many *amoreuses* was the nymph Mentha, who gave her name to the mint family.) The juice from

bitter aloe (aloe vera) is a powerful purgative, and gel from its
fleshy leaves makes a soothing lotion for sunburned skin: Scorpios'
pale skin is usually sensitive to the Sun. Witch hazel, also called
winterbloom because its flowers appear on bare stems in late
autumn after its leaves have fallen, is still prescribed as an
external remedy for bruises. Scorpios need to ensure the free flow
of their body systems, and can benefit from herbal preparations
(bryony, furze and broom) that aid digestion and respiratory
functions. Hops are reputed to have properties that cleanse the
blood, and they also brew the real ale of which many a Scorpio
is a connoisseur.

THE CELESTIAL BODY

ach part of the body comes under the influence of a different zodiac sign. Appropriately for this intense and passionate sign, Scorpio rules the sexual organs, the parts of the body that oversee the creation and generation of life. Scorpio's planetary ruler, Pluto, is also associated with the reproductive processes.

The rhythm of life must flow unimpeded through Scorpio, and any disruption to the flow, physical or psychological, can cause health problems. Scorpios should not allow themselves to brood, submit to stress, or bottle up bad or powerful emotions for too

long. Rich foods, which Scorpio adores, should be reasonably rationed. As the part of the body ruled by the polar sign also figures in health matters, every Scorpio should take care of throat and neck, ruled by Taurus.

Scorpio has an extremely high level of energy, which must be burned off to prevent frustration. Martial arts, with their rigid discipline and emphasis on the power of the mind, might be suitable exercise. Fencing, the high energy *danse macabre* involving cold steel, iron nerve and incisive cunning is an ideal Scorpionic sport. After a hard day duelling with the world, intense Scorpio will enjoy a bath spiced with exotic oils of ginger, or cinnamon, or a long, slow massage with oil of mandarin or neroli.

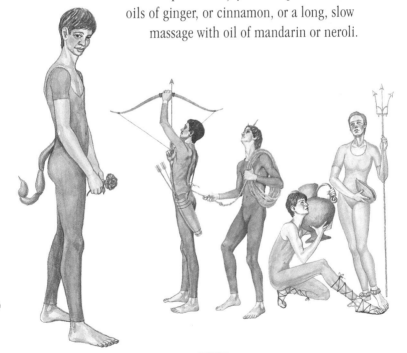

THE STARS AND THE STONES

Runes are a code, secret keys to the different facets of the whole interconnecting universe. Originated by the Germanic nomads who wandered the plains of northern Italy some 500 years before Christ, this compact and portable form of magic crossed the Alps and spread throughout northern Europe and Scandinavia. The twenty-four 'letters' of the *futharc* (an acronym of the first six letters of the runic alphabet) were used by the pragmatic Germans as a straightforward recording medium as well as a shortcut to tapping the secrets of the universe. Each rune is a powerpacked symbol of one aspect of existence – for example, the fourth rune *As* means ash tree, but also signifies the tree of the world, the divine force that controls the cosmic order.

When the runes are cast, they combine, and the trained runemaster can read what has been, what is, and what influences are shaping future events. Authentic ancient runes, the portable arkana, were carved or painted on fresh-cut fruitwood and cast onto a white cloth for divination, but pebble or stone runes work just as well. Everyone should make their own runes – they have personal power, and they are free.

Runic astrology divides the sky into twenty-four segments, or seles, which correspond with the futharc. The seles modify the expression of the planetary energy as each planet passes through them. The planets carry the attributes of the northern gods, and these too have runic associations.

As the sun signs do not coincide with the runic seles, they often come under the influence of two or more runes. The Scorpio runes are *Wyn*, *Hagal* and *Nyd*. *Wyn* means joy, in Scorpio's case the determination and zest for success. *Hagel*, meaning hail, the most important rune for Scorpio, is very complex: it signifies the ability to impose rigidity and shape on the essentially amorphous, to control external events by willpower. It is also a symbol of the indivisible powers of destruction and regeneration – hail falls to earth as a hard, icy, crop-devastating shower, then melts into water that refreshes the very crops it has damaged. *Nyd*, another complex rune, means need, in this case the need to 'know thyself', to achieve independence, to understand one's own motives; *Nyd* also brings intensity to any action or emotion. The runic image of Scorpio – determined, intense, powerful, at once destructive and creative, possessed of a Svengali-like force of will, very self-assured but an enigma to everyone else – is remarkably similar to the zodiacal profile.

Scorpio's planetary ruler Pluto is equivalent to the northern deities Villi and Vé (elimination and regeneration), the younger brothers of Odin. Pluto's associated runes are *Rad*, literally wheel, or riding, signifying conscious control over transformation, and *Eoh*, the yew, a powerful defence against death and destruction. As Scorpio was traditionally ruled by Mars, perhaps the Mars rune *Tir* (sword) may shed some oblique runic light. *Tir* signifies directed energy, justified assertion, the aim and will to succeed.

S C O R P I O
ZODIAC TREASURE

he zodiac treasure hoard may overflow with gorgeous gems, but it is guarded by grumpy and confused dragons, who squabble among themselves and cannot agree on which stone best fits which sign. However, the beguiling idea of a jewelled girdle encircling the zodiac is an ancient one, and may even be based on the twelve gemstones, one for each of the tribes of Israel, set on the breastplate of the Jewish high priests of biblical times. Medieval astrologers felt reasonably sure of their ground and listed the gems as follows, in zodiacal order: bloodstone, sapphire, agate, emerald,

onyx, carnelian, chrysolite, aquamarine, topaz, ruby, garnet and amethyst. Catherine de Medici, the original power-dresser, was rumoured to possess a glittering belt of zodiacal gems.

As there is no real concensus in the matter, a new approach is needed. Consideration of the colour and characteristics traditionally attributed to each sun sign may lead to a satisfying match of sign with stone.

The Scorpio colour is dark red: burgundy, oxblood, maroon. Wine-dark garnets look very handsome on Scorpio women, who have the necessary panache to carry off a *parure* – a matching set of necklace, earrings, bracelets and tiara. Garnets also pack a crystal punch, revitalizing the spirit and focusing the passions.

Technically, Scorpio could lay legitimate claim to every jewel in the chest, as Pluto, Scorpio's ruler, commands all the precious stones and mineral wealth of the underworld. For instance, intuitive scorpions might wear beryls, which Egyptians called the seer's stone, or opals; but opals need care as they allegedly bring down the vengeance of Venus on cheating hearts, always a risk with highly charged Scorpio. Male Scorpios are enthusiastic plutocrats when it comes to jewellery, going well beyond the timid display of cufflinks to flaunting dramatic neck chains, earrings and even nose studs.

When buying jewellery for Scorpio, look at the dramatic and unusual: glass and steel gothic, sculptural pieces, jewellery made from unlikely materials, bejewelled insect brooches, rings set with stones like eyeballs, replicas of the chrome and steel costume jewellery of the 1940s. It's difficult to go over the top when decorating scorpions.

S C O R P I O
EARTH'S HIDDEN POWER

eneath the earth, in the realm of Pluto, lie the solidified energies, metals and crystals that hum with compacted potency. Scorpios can choose between steel and iron as their special metal. Tough, valiant iron belongs to Scorpio's traditional ruler, Mars. Scorpio admires iron's rigid discipline; wrought or cast, it resolutely holds its patterns. But steel, an alloy of iron and carbon, is more versatile, producing engines of destruction as well as machineries of joy: swords, knives, bayonets and guns are balanced by ploughshares, cooking pots, trains, boats, planes and cars. Scorpios are possessed of a steely-eyed gaze as famous as their nerves of steel, and they like to surround themselves with their favourite metal as much as possible. Wealthy Scorpios (of whom there are many) might display antique edged weapons on the wall; they will certainly keep a state-of-the-art automobile in the garage. Gourmet scorpions' kitchens will be equipped with the very best stainless-steel cooking pots. And Scorpios may favour

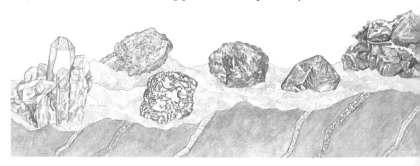

dramatic steel and black leather furniture: they are probably the only members of the zodiac who could appreciate the surreal cold comfort of a stainless-steel armchair.

Crystals are chemical elements compressed over millenia into dense, solid form, storehouses of electromagnetic energy. Scorpio can claim red and green jasper, the crystals that alert you to deception, and force you to peer deeper into the reality of your surroundings and the loyalty of your friends; opal, the 'eye-stone' which strengthens Scorpio's eagle eyes and enhances intuitive powers; and the garnet, which helps to harmonize and balance physical and emotional passions. Scorpio's ruler, Pluto, has mysterious tektite, the uncompromising black crystal born from dead meteorites, a gloomy indicator of negative influences. A more cheerful crystalline echo comes from Mars, Scorpio's traditional ruler, who brings the positive energies of citrine quartz, the detoxifier and enemy to self-destruction; and agate, the crystal that enhances strength and courage in body and mind.

Each crystal is an individual, and you must always choose your own. Take your time, pick up those that attract you and handle them gently to find the one that uniquely suits you.

SCORPIO ON THE CARDS

ometimes called the Devil's Picture Book, the tarot was probably created in the twelfth century, but its origins are suitably shrouded in secrecy. There are seventy-eight cards: twenty-two in the Major Arcana, a gallery of enigmatic archetypal images from the Fool via the Wheel of Fortune to the World, and fifty-six in the Minor Arcana, divided into four suits – coins, cups, swords and batons (or wands).

Tarot cards, being one of the ways to explore the human psyche, have an affinity with the zodiac sun signs, and cards from the Major Arcana and the court cards from the Minor Arcana are

associated with specific signs. If two cards are assigned they should be considered together, but in some cases only one is appropriate.

To Scorpio falls the Devil, the fifteenth card in the Major Arcana, a macabre, rather alarming card sometimes called the Black Magician. Like most things to do with Scorpio, it is complex and disturbing: the Devil is androgynous, forcing us to recognize the male and female elements in ourselves; he/she stands over two demons, the carnal urges, loosely chained, ready to run riot at any moment. This card signifies the need for total self-awareness, the recognition that the shadowy, untamed, instinctual side of ourselves – the Edward Hyde to our Henry Jekyll – is as significant as our civilized selves. Only then can the power of the dark forces be harnessed for good, instinct tamed by intellect: the Devil carries a bright-bladed sword (or a flaming torch), the beacon of conscience to light the way through the labyrinthine regions of our darker selves.

Scorpio's ruler Pluto is associated with Death, probably the most terrifying card in the pack. Less fearsome than it appears, it means change: inevitable, irresistible, the essential for progress or new growth. Without change, there is stagnation: and that is true death.

There are many ways to lay out the tarot cards for a reading, but a particularly zodiacal one is to place the significator (the card chosen to represent the questioner) in the centre and lay out the other cards in a circle anticlockwise, starting from the nine-o-clock position. This follows the layout of the astrological Houses, and the cards are interpreted in the context of the House in which they fall.

INDEX